STRANGELY HAPPY

Joan Margarit was born in 1938 in Sanaüja, La Segarra region, in Catalonia. He is an architect, and from 1968 until his retirement was also Professor of Structural Calculations at Barcelona's Technical School of Architecture. He first published poetry in Spanish, in 1963 and 1965, but after a silence of ten years switched to writing and publishing in Catalan. From 1980 he began to establish his reputation as a leading Catalan poet. As well as publishing many collections in Catalan, he has translated most of his own books into Spanish. He has published two editions of his Catalan poetry translated into English by Anna Crowe, both published by Bloodaxe Books: *Tugs in the Fog: Selected Poems* (2006) and *Strangely Happy* (2011). *Tugs in the Fog* was the first translation into English of his Catalan poetry, and a Poetry Book Society Recommended Translation.

JOAN MARGARIT

STRANGELY HAPPY

TRANSLATED BY
ANNA CROWE

BLOODAXE BOOKS

ISBN: 978 1 85224 893 2

First published 2011 by
Bloodaxe Books Ltd,
Highgreen,
Tarset,
Northumberland NE48 1RP.

www.bloodaxebooks.com
For further information about Bloodaxe titles
please visit our website or write to
the above address for a catalogue.

Supported by
**ARTS COUNCIL
ENGLAND**

Cover design: Neil Astley & Pamela Robertson-Pearce.

Printed in Great Britain by
Bell & Bain Limited, Glasgow, Scotland.

For Racquel

ACKNOWLEDGEMENTS

Strangely Happy is a translation of poems selected from two collections by Joan Margarit, *Casa de Misericòrdia* (2007) and *Misteriosament feliç* (2008), both published by Col. Óssa Menor, Enciclopèdia Catalana, Barcelona. The translation of this work was supported by a grant from the Institut Ramon Llull.

 institut
ramon llull
Catalan Language and Culture

CONTENTS

On the evening of the day on which I had seen Miss Scatcherd flog her pupil, Burns, I wandered as usual among the forms and tables and laughing groups without a companion, yet not feeling lonely […] I looked out; it snowed fast, a drift was already forming against the lower panes; putting my ear close to the window, I could distinguish from the gleeful tumult within, the disconsolate moan of the wind outside.

CHARLOTTE BRONTË: *Jane Eyre*

He's a lucky man who loves this silence
of the written word and is able to have
a girl with eyes the colour of wood
so as to grow old together.

J.M.: *The first frosts*

from

CASA DE MISERICÒRDIA

The orchid hunter

At home there were scarcely any books
fit for adolescent restlessness.
The essays on town planning bored me
and *Catalonia, an unlucky people*
was too sad a title.
I picked up *Mein Kampf,* a small black book
that seemed profound to me. I made my début,
via the filthiest spot in literature.
Hitler's words, utterly vulgar,
revealed a dark pit.
I haven't forgotten it in spite of not remembering it.
I was lucky to bump into reality.
That is where poetry began,
difficult, with no false hopes.
I have always done what the wild boar does,
who searches for and, delicately, selects and eats
the bulb, of what is known as the *orchis,* of the orchid.

The assassin's gear

Among the disasters piled up like sacks,
life has left me your love.
Neither the silence of the night,
nor the black car with its lights off
nor the sax heard, softly, on the radio
are of any importance.
What must be faultless is the aim:
dangerous and sure. Like you in my life.

Being old

Among the shades of those cocks and dogs
of the courtyards and farmyards of Sanaüja,
there is a pit of lost time and dirty rain
that sees children march against death.
Being old is a kind of post-war time.
I see those who loved me
seated around the kitchen table
sifting lentils on evenings beside the brazier.
So poor that at the end of that war
they had to sell the wretched
patch of vineyard and the icy farmhouse.
Being old means that the war is over.
Knowing where the shelters are, now useless.

Prozac

The moon is an ice cube in the glass of darkness
that life offers me. What story
does not attempt to deny its murky epilogue?
But it is I who am the monster, and no other person
whom, to save myself, I can kill.
Life is precisely this disaster.
How to root out the blame of the stones?
How to stop the pain inside a tunnel?
How to hear, so far off in the night,
whether our dead daughter is crying?
Antidepressants are pesticides.
The endings of fairytales are always untrue,
so children do not take their own lives.

Etymologies

It is my weakness that conquers you,
the purest essence of suffering.
We were so young when we first met,
but already I opened this wound in you:
a door through which each time you go
further away and so come back later and later.
Love comes from impulse,
from to rape and torture. From to ride.

The first time

We met in Plaça Catalunya,
in front of the row of clocks
that marked the timetable of the cities of the world.
I have not yet ceased to laugh or weep over you.
The moon has always been in the cold glass
of the windows of our life
like one of those clocks, which now mark
the past and future of our love.
In some city of the mind
I shall be loving you
when your lonely hour is marked
by the moon's face over the sea.

Church

I have come inside into the silence and the half-light.
I sit down on the hardness of one of the benches.
The fear of death impregnates every arch
like the smoke that gradually darkens the ceiling
above a fireplace down the years.
I hear children's voices singing,
muffled behind the thickness of the walls.
A ray of sun crosses the vast empty space.
I fear children's songs
now, as much as churches.

As a concert begins

Embarked on the music,
I sail away from reality's quayside
into a dark sea.
Exhilarated, I think I know where it is carrying me.
Restlessly, the mind that wants to follow it
bangs like a fly against a pane of glass.
With the seats in darkness,
the orchestra is moving like a vessel
with all lights blazing in the night.

Suite

He has got up early and is sitting
in the living-room. It is still dark.
He remembers when Lluís Claret played
here for the three of them, for him and the two others,
who listened from this sofa
where now he waits for dawn to begin.
Like a siren sounding in a port,
the cello was saying goodbye to the girl
with the second *Suite* by Bach.

Your mother and I are growing old,
but that is something you'll never have to see,
the man says, while he gazes out at the courtyard.
A bird is already singing when he has put on
that piece, played by Lluís,
and once more he has felt against his chest
the gentle weight of Joana's head.
Now, when it is already beginning to grow light,
in her generosity she has returned
in the *Suite for cello* – the second –
which is, since she died, the way she comes home.

Riera

Canalised and dry,
it runs through the village and into the sea
with its floor and walls of concrete
broad and white in the moonlight.
The banks, above the walls, among the reeds,
are thick with fennel and broom.
Every so often, a dark waft
is silently graced by the lighted
windows among the orchards.
I walk along the *riera* to the beach.
No streets or paths, just the naked
and forlorn amplitude awaiting
the flood's brutal and furious waters.

Riera is the common river bed peculiar to Mediterranean coasts.
They are usually dry, but when it rains heavily they fill and pour
down with rushing waters that carry off out to sea anything in
their path. In modern times they have been canalised, with floor
and both banks made of reinforced concrete.

House of Mercy

The father, shot.
Or, as the judge says, executed.
The mother, poverty and hunger,
the petition someone types out for her:
Saludo al Vencedor, Segundo Año Triunfal,
Solicito a Vuecencia to have my children
put in the *Casa de la Misericòrdia.*

The coldness of their future is in a petition.
The orphanages and hospices were harsh,
but the weather was harsher.
True charity is frightening.
It is like poetry: a good poem,
however beautiful, has to be cruel.
There is nothing else. Poetry is now
the final orphanage, the last house of mercy.

'House of Mercy' is the literal translation of the Catalan and means
an orphanage.
Lines 5-6: In Castilian in the Catalan original: *Hail to the Conqueror,*
Second Year of Triumph, I beseech your worship... Fascistic and rhetorical
post-war language. Franco prohibited all use of the Catalan language.

Stacking wood

The man habitually goes to the wood to pick up
the trunks that have fallen after a storm.
He stacks them behind the house.
In the case of each one he remembers
what made it fall and where he picked it up.
On cold nights, as he gazes at the flames,
he burns what is left of what he loves.

Raquel's good sense

It is now five years since Joana died:
five years he has been running away. He phones me
from cities abroad. He is alone
and during this time he has aged.
He should have stayed at home, I think.
We would be together now. We would talk,
though we wouldn't speak of the future.
Only from time to time, looking through the window
at the dark green of the courtyard, one of us
would say with a sigh: winter is coming.

Citizens

I hail from a colder time. Before dawn,
frosty paths carried silent shadows
to the factories' big filthy windows.
Today those shadows from the past
that deafened the world with their songs
look out from inside me.
They don't understand a thing.
They gaze at an opulent poverty
that doesn't even know it is poverty.
It's the end of a dream. Nowadays art
must be democratic. No tall trees.
Terrifyingly rich and, for that reason,
terrifyingly poor.

Advice

Become an old man and make her become old as well
(letter from Hemingway to Dos Passos)

It is pointless advice, because sex
induces the same fear when you become old
as when you are young, the same fear
as when you were a child, and dogs mated
and people kicked them
and they, stuck together, yelping with pain,
ran away down the dusty street of the village.
Where the waves die
I see once more your feet from when you were a young woman
polished by the slow and peaceable water.

The rose seller

Furtive and solitary, the man with bouquets
goes round the night spots, looking for couples.
I came across him in the streets near the Rambla
with some roses that have no rose scent
on a night that does not smell of night.
I have lost myself in the back streets of life.
In the darkness a woman who is not you
has stolen your eyes and is weeping. The city
is a precise and monstrous replica.
As if Cupid had become an old man,
the rose seller goes by, spitting.
While he disappears I think: you forgive
your love nothing. Not even its ending.

Couple

There is a city of melancholy ironwork
under a brigands' red moon,
as in marriages made for love.
The lights of an attic, with the rusty
remains of some youthful treasure,
shine out in the night. It is a hard
pornography of an abrupt old man whose hand
she now holds while she smiles
deceiving him for the last time.
There is a city of melancholy ironwork.
He still goes back to meet up with her
in the bourgeois cafés which a cynical,
brutal and Catalan indifference
was gradually destroying. Now, what does it matter.
Love has meant crossing this magnificent bridge
to reach the other side of a dried-up river.

Tram

It has grown dark. In the rain, the cars
come home to their garages. My father
never came home in a car.
In galoshes and mackintosh, he stepped down
off a tram, one of those iron ones
that still rumble through my brain.
He always came home and I do not know
how to come home to where my daughter is.

In a small village

Dark rooms at ground level in a narrow street:
out of them comes the sound of a hammer and dust from rubble.
Through the gap of the doorway I can just make out
a man on his own, breaking something up, and an old man
standing nearby, watching him. They do not speak,
as though both were listening to the blows
of a grief that only they recognise.
Now the doorway devours my gaze
and drags it fiercely inside.
If I were to approach them, they might not even hear me.
This is the slow, interminable work
that goes on inside the house, where no one watches.

Winter before daybreak

I remember them from when I was a child: the huge
brightly-lit doors of the market would open –
as though they were my mother, who wasn't there –
in the dark frost of the street
along which I walked, fearfully, to school.
Do all the fears of the old
come from the dark streets of childhood?
Mother, the brightly-lit door,
for a child you left too long on his own.

Crematorium

Burning the dead has an aura of night
with fire and the smell of smoke
among vivid garments that flutter like flags
on the bank of a wide, reddish river.
But this cold and ugly mortuary,
its smoke devoid of any image or smell,
does not even bring gusts of dry leaves
to empty shoes. My Ganges
cuts across the memory of a flat
near the Rambla when, in the small hours,
the street lights bathe it in gloom.
Now that you are both dead, inside me
there is a splinter of light under a door,
as though you were about to go to bed.

Saturn

You ripped up my books of poems
and threw them out of the window into the street.
The pages looked like rare butterflies
that were floating down on people.
I don't know whether we might, now,
be able to understand each other,
two tired and disappointed old men.
Probably not. Let's leave it as it is.
You wanted to devour me. I wanted to kill you.
Me, the son you had during the war.

Widow

In my feminine high heels I rise up
towards rage, my eyes write for you
with a scrawl the name of my lover.
What's left of you and me is a pit full of dead birds.
When I was little they would shut me in a wardrobe:
now I wait in the darkness of a cinema
for the child of failure
to stop crying inside me.
What you never told me is this coldness.
What I never told you are the stones
oblivion hurls from the beach into the sea.
In my feminine high heels I rise up
changed, raging, sensual,
and I look down, towards your grave.

Diaries (1937-1944)

Across the yellow, dried-out pages
of the pocket diaries of those years
their handwriting runs, his and hers,
tiny, using up every bit of space
between the day of the month, the week,
and the names of saints' days.
Dazzling and luminous, there unfolds
the passion for being alive. Even
among the refuse of fear.
They used writing as a way of being together,
in spite of empty cupboards, hopeless
as the coffins of the war, and those trains,
crowded, dirty, slow, that kept them apart.
They tried to escape those years
with words of love, covering with moss
the rocks against which afterwards life,
harder than the war, shattered them.

Because intimacy is like a cellar,
they always hid these diaries.
Today their love, like republican
currency at the end of the war,
is no longer legal tender.
It is worth nothing to them.
The past returns, but life
has already unmasked it.

Marriott Hotel

It is raining in your eyes while, in the windows,
as if it were a compass in the night,
the Chrysler's needle lights up, shining
on top of the most beautiful skyscraper in the world.
The rain is falling asleep with your name,
cleansing the black well of melancholy.
The emergency sirens cut across
tunnels of alarm in the empty streets.
They are deafening voices from the past
telling me to stop and go home.
Nothingness at the needle's frozen north.

Chess

Memory is fraying
like the snapped cables of boats
that the storm has carried off.
Understanding is tiring. But never too much so,
because it cannot be the final refuge.
We are the king and queen in a difficult
endgame on a board that now has few pieces.

Behind the door

For many years we would rise before dawn
to make ready her breakfast and her clothes.
I made this pact with insomnia, this mark
of solitude similar to that which came to me
from broken toys in childhood.
I still rise before it begins to get light,
and memories come down the empty streets.
I make up somewhere I'm going, and on the pavement,
in front of the house, I listen: like a dog,
death is scratching behind the door.

The children's home

León, 1970

Beneath the blue and icy sky of Castile,
as though hope had cut through
the rain of the night, I hear their voices
and I see them playing in the yard.
The winter sun
caresses them like a mother.
With poorhouse-coloured eyes they gaze into the future,
which is an empty pool, but their feet
jump happily over the puddles of blue rain
which reflect a sky
that this winter morning promises them life.

Walking into a story

Over the wood in silence falls the snow,
a thick blanket which does not warm
the wretched multitude of oaks.
Well wrapped-up, I cross it on foot:
where the path was it has stayed covered
and the only tracks left are my steps.
I come upon a fallen nest, a very large nest
as though it were the cradle of a dead child.
Now, to go back the way I came, I need
my own footprints, but the snow
is falling and keeps silently wiping them out.
A gust of wind sets up a disturbance
and the nest is dragged along, bowling
through dumb, cold weather, with no paths.

Plans

His friend showed him over the house
and which partition walls he wanted to pull down,
and which doorways to open in the supporting walls.
And he told him he should do nothing,
since houses have never saved anyone.
You're attracted to ruins, he told him.
Lying to yourself until you fall, engrossed and frozen,
in your bedroom of deception,
where you imagine her smiling.

And then he fell silent, as birds do
when they hear footsteps too close to where they sing.

Encounters

Sometimes in very lonely places,
like an airport bar or the berth
of a night train,
a wave of sadness wraps itself round me.
It means she is passing close by me,
and that she is walking determinedly away,
supporting herself on her crutches, to the end of time.

Coldness of June at Forès

It was the landscape of our life:
the flight of steps made of green terraces
under the vigilance of the wind,
and on the highest one, indifferent, the village.
Fierce swifts swathe
the empty house in the threads of their flight.
They scream unceasingly. Dark, gleaming,
they make a noise like knives. Like this swift,
still flying at dusk, there remains for us too
a remote possibility.
It is, already, the landscape of our death.
Under the vigilance of the wind.

Andorra Park Hotel

The man reads insomnia in the dark pane.
Here, where later they built the hotel,
that lad concealed beneath a stone
a love letter and made a map,
the real map of a treasure.
But the treasure was an act of cowardice:
the words he didn't dare to say to a girl.
His final love-letter,
that he did indeed put into her hand.
Then the cowardice or the contempt –
he will never know – came from a woman.
Dawn was approaching the hotel windows
like a warship.
No woman remembers any letter.
The clouds forecast cold and snow.

Girls

Memory needs to utter some name
in order to live with what it fears.
He thinks of her: he began to lose her
when he embraced her that first night.
The man breaks open the past like a money-box
and inside there was nothing but darkness.
In time's bones there is no tenderness.
The places no longer exist.
Girls are now either old or dead.

Children's voices

The future in my eyes is a sad grey,
a film of tired light in which to remember
their bedtimes. The story books
with hard covers and bright colours,
I still read them in that room,
in the light from the bedside lamp.
There are early mornings when, suddenly,
I hear a child calling me and I sit up,
but there is no one, only an old man
who has heard the murmur of memory,
a light rustle of air in the dark
as though a bullet passed through the house.
Turning out the light meant keeping a treasure safe.

Railway sadness

The moon in the windows on one side
of the restaurant car. Desperate,
running like a fanatic along the rails
of the brutal wounds of the past,
the night train gleams like a horse
at full gallop covered in sweat.
I hear its hooves crossing the iron bridges
as it cuts across your death.
Wherever I go, there is always your death:
it is now a black mirror which the locomotive
carries before it and confronts it with its hell.
No one now weeps for you, there remains
not a single handkerchief waving on any platform.
I am this night train that is searching, wherever
it might be, for the wheelchair in the night.

Horizon

A plain of yellow stubble fields.
Like a line drawn on a plan,
the motorway goes all the way to the horizon.
I think that I too am tracing
a steady line on my life.
Far from a built-up and ugly coast,
with the window down, I drive
feeling the air on my face, inland.

Father

He kept a place for me beside him
on a train that was vanishing on the horizon.

I remember him coming closer, defenceless, at the end.
Although, in suit and tie,
he seemed as if he were giving orders.
He was very frightened. Very. And yet,
he conveyed a new dignity
as he took, in his elegance, the final bend.

I am aware of the danger as I walk past mirrors;
aware, on the dismal stony ground of childhood,
of where it lies hidden, the viper of his love.

Vineyards of Solivella

I am walking between two names.
The fields after the grape harvest
are a tomb of air where now I write
Joana and *Marta* with my eyes. The afternoon,
ungrudgingly, is growing dark
and covers both names while memories
cling like moss to the bark.
Dead farmers ride on the old tractors
that make no sound now as they pass through the fields.
Yellowish headlamps that shed no light move forward
crossing the dark-green gold that towards nightfall
glazes November vines.

Lake song

Solitary lake wearing
the chill of your water
with no love there:
your silence betrays you.

Your lake's chill
is freezing my water.
With no love there.
My silence betrays you.

Because I too am still,
your water is my water.
With no love there.
Your silence betrays me.

Like you, I wear in my eyes
the chill of my water.
With no love there.
My silence betrays me.

Shostakovitch, 'Leningrad' Symphony

Do you remember? Joana had died.
You and I were going north by car,
to the flat that faces the sea,
and we listened to this symphony.
We began the journey
on a luminous morning. In the music
the day was made of walls covered in ice,
shadows of passers-by with half-empty sacks
and sledges with corpses on the lake.
Like a runway in the sun,
the motorway ran onwards and, behind the sounds,
there stretched the fog from the howitzers
and tank tracks in the snow.
It was a blue-gold July morning
sparkling on the crystal sea.
In the brass and strings was the echo
of glory, which is always in the past,
rejecting, always rejecting, life.
At night all that was left was the murmur
of the waves below the terrace.
In us, though, just as in the music,
there raged the storm of snow and iron
that is unleashed when a page of history turns.

Applying Greek tragedy

The future, before it happens, never looks like it,
but when it is already here there is always someone
saying, *Something terrible is happening.*
Somewhere perhaps you are already lost.
There are thoughts that today are already present:
all it needs is for hatred to intensify like the fires
started in the dark windy nights of summer,
while in your bed you're asleep, deeply asleep
with an innocence that is, unfailingly, stupid.

Light of my life

I was a boy who used to listen to love songs
on the radio, and there was nothing
I liked looking at more than women.
What bliss
the mist of their bodies in the street
and all the dreams in which I unclothed them.
I can remember the brutal erection
of a boy who was abandoned under the rain,
the premonition of the old man I am.
I like to remember the body of the girl
who stayed with me. I still hear
her happy voice over the telephone:
Give the children their supper. I'll be back late.
In all probability, she never came back,
but now that we're old it's all the same to us.

The final game

Girls and boys play: *that's home.*
That's a castle. Here, it's a desert island.
And they point to a place. They need nothing else.
The trimmings come later.
Once again I say, pointing to an abstract place
like that of childhood: *that's home.*
And all places are nothing but death.

Winter drought

With no frost on the hard ground,
with the black ice the birds disappear.
Beneath the blue sky, shining and tearless,
the morning air is a magnifying glass.
Dark purple in colour on the horizon,
the mountains come closer like blame.

'How I have to build'

That was what that clear, sensible book was called
from which so many architects of my day
learned our trade. And the author
was an architect and likewise a poet.
I read his *Sonnet to Joana*,
in which there are these innocent, terrible lines:
Oh Joana whom the sea carried off one day
towards enormous, many-coloured America...
How should a wall be bonded? How should a daughter
be shrouded? Or what is the pitch
I should give a roof? My Joana
was carried off by death, as though by a dark sea,
towards another, deep America.
Out of so much architecture there remains only
the loneliness of the wall. Its strength.
I am looking at it in the courtyard where Joana
used to smile at me. Now I do not have to build.

Chemotherapy

It has to begin today.
Before dawn she is awake
in the darkness of the bedroom.
The darkness will win, she thinks:
the black sun in the black dawn
will rise in the black city
with its dark port by a dark sea.
She knows it because inside her
there is a guest she does not understand,
abstract of darkness.
To rest she needs the blackness
of eyes tight shut,
and outside is dark, and the room
is as dark as her mind.
In her mind sadness grows.
In the sadness, fear.
When the shutters are opened,
a red sun comes through the glass,
grievous and brutal.

Slippers

To get up, first he sits on the edge of the bed
and, looking at his thin, white feet,
pushes them into his slippers.
The smiling portraits are waking up.
He stretches out his hand to the confused past,
and feels between the sheets that woman
who has for years now been someone else.
He feels the warmth in his feet, which makes him think
of what he always called a great love.

Perspective

Behind the dark window panes are the fir trees,
black, motionless, as though they were princes,
on Christmas Eve. It is snowing.
The reflection of the flames in the hearth
goes on caressing us with an unseen hand.
It is a memory, it lies, because things
in life do not happen as in stories.
In spite of that, memories are useful,
because in this way we dream that the dead,
our dead, accompany us.
You have yours. I mine.
But the girl is from both.
Each of us stands on either side of a tomb.

The last drink

When he walks under the red neon lights into the bar,
the man thinks of the lights of the railway tracks.
Standing at the counter he drinks down
the black and purple alcohol of a rainy past.
He tries to go back home, but the rusty
lock no longer opens. He drops
the keys on the pavement among the motorcycles.
Just below him, the drain with its rats
is the silence of the neighbourhood's fear
of the ineluctable future that is here already.

The cobbler

We used to play there with a football.
The church square was raised up
a couple of metres above some small gardens
that were beside a cobbler's shop.
When the ball dropped down there, one of us
had to go quickly scrambling down.
If the cobbler got there before us,
he would slash it with his knife.
I don't know whose throat he was cutting
in the boys' rubber ball. He frightened me.
A fear that was not at all the same as the fear
of fairytales or being locked in my room in the dark.
It was a harder fear. More real.
Like when you went off with someone else,
or when our daughter died.

Cemetery and sea

His father built this cemetery
at the entrance to the village, among the pine trees.
He was a good architect, the man thinks to himself
as he approaches the stony beach
and the dark and transparent rocking of the sea.
The sea is tied down. It tightens, will be in force
when the storms come as though it were trying
to uproot the chains of its bed.
That is loneliness, the man thinks to himself now,
chained to we know not what,
holding on to obsessions, pain and mistakes
within a bitter dark transparency.
When you are young it is easy to share the future.
Now, the past smells
of rottenness, diesel, salt.
Smells of the sea. And of loneliness.
The village runs from the cemetery to the sea.

Divorced

The house overlooks a street
where no one is waiting for me.
Here, without you. A stranger.

Here is where I have strayed.
Without me I walk with you.
My shadow is a mistake
that comes from the iciest places:
your heart, your hands.
That is why I went away.

The unknown life
I have lived without you.
At your side.

Still life

The hunter is blinded by the beating of wings
or the thunder of hooves on the ground.
He falls exhausted with walking,
the animals' warm blood smearing
the fur, the feathers, and his hands.
There is nothing poetic in poetry.
The gold of these dead eyes tells him autumn
is nothing more than mud weighing down his shoes,
the game's stench in the days that follow
and those who will be round the table to eat it all up
with no thought for him, or how this old
and futile ritual is killing him.

The chill of the sea

Such a longing to touch her face.
This summer no one has spoken her name.
What you haven't wept for, you won't weep for
in the autumn of fallen leaves and roses.
Just as though this were about lost illusions,
the waves come in, tame and grey,
forming words that tell me only
what it was that mattered and matters no longer.
As though she were still there,
I am suddenly dazzled, brutally, as though
by lightning, by the *braille* of this sea.

Luggage

When we're going on a journey, your mother and I
pack our cases on top of your bed.
Neatly folded clothes, toiletries,
books, tickets, medicines,
scattered but in order.
All journeys begin here,
in this spacious and intimate room
that we painted a soft fuchsia
knowing you were never coming back.
The room has put forth roots which, bit by bit,
go deeper and deeper into your absence.
We pack our cases for a night train.

Portrait of a girl

(Balthus: Thérèse, *1938. Metropolitan Museum, New York)*

The old man stops in front of the painting and looks
at the bare legs, one lying on top of the other,
and the experienced childish face.
Letting herself flop in the chair, she
shows not even the beginning of a smile.

The man feels that the rosy, naked skin
of her inner thigh can save him.
Some children's story is being burnt
to the left in front of him, like a poisoned
puddle towards which the girl is looking
in order not to look at him, who is horrified
by motherhood and by lust.

Gazing at the stars

It comes from a blurred imaginary past
made from the dust of shining molecules
in the bloody deltas of the brain.
The mind is the path that leads towards death.
I would show the angel. I would tell him
that the tiny flame of a candle
makes the shadow of the room more enormous,
or the shadow of the house, desert, or forest,
or whatever the huge and frozen place may be
that I try to imagine as welcoming.

The orphan

She was lost, he was lost. There remained
what there was behind tenderness:
that darkness behind the wings
of the guardian angel.
They were hot and ordinary days
growing grimy with tears like fat
drops falling on dusty paths.
No guardian angel, then.
She was lost, he was lost: orphaned
by their own daughter in the hospice
with the broken windows of life's end.

Evening falls on the Dead Sea

In the delicate blue and pink
of water and mountains there is a memory
of those scripture lessons.
You, poisonous lake, are my childhood,
salt sea of Bible stories,
stagnant water which, when I tasted it,
burned my gums and my tongue,
like the prayers that they made me learn.
They wanted to turn me into that sea,
that has no opening, into an abstract
mind, confined by the desert.
They are all dead now, and I grow old
admiring the monstrous beauty
of a sea with no port. With no boat.

Still

Let me look into your eyes and sink
into the hot and dark imagining
of seeing you naked in another's arms.
These are not the whims of the old. Nor deviance.
It is the hard, ruddy-black stone
of the peach I ate in my hunger,
which still I scour with my tongue
preserving the sweetness of your love.

Barcelona final love

Absence is a house
with its radiators frozen.
I come from there. A long path
as far as this final love.
Like the violent summer
when in September it rests.

In the twilight of the port
another city sinks
in a sea that is weary of light.
And the final city remains,
where I shall find nobody
whom I can ask.
I am walking into it
with pigeons grimy with sadness
that vanish into trees or on to roofs
when evening comes.
They are like us: nor
do they have melodious voices
to escape from death,
that little square
we are approaching
along our usual streets.

Happiness

Your life goes onward within me,
and I sing you all the love songs
I can still remember: torn *boleros*
that reason has already turned into tombs,
romantic *lieder* like putrescence
that can shine in the dark,
desire curdling in the cancerous throat
of the French *chanson*. I sing
in the wind of lost arias
the cradle songs that are holes
in childhood's wretched counterpane.
I sing to you but no one knows it.
They don't know why I am an old man singing.

The sea wall

There is a man standing right in front of the dock.
After the storm, with losses taken on board
and huge, wandering griefs now moored,
the best place to wait is the harbour.
The harbour is like he is now: inside him,
enormous, at rest, the sea and the ships.

from

MISTERIOSAMENT FELIÇ

Saying goodbye

I have removed rugs and curtains,
all the tables where for some time now
I neither eat nor write.
I have taken down the pictures and painted the walls
to erase the marks of so many years.
I have kept a few books. I know which ones they are.
I have destroyed love letters.
Silent, now, each love
is a wandering iceberg of my thought.
With no corners left for fear,
the house has left my eyes naked.
Not even hope will trouble the final death.
There is no other house for those I love.

Lost city

Homage to Thomas Hardy

It was early morning, dark and cold,
when I left the bar where the lights
were already being switched off, in an area
of wretched streets. The city
was like the corpse of my life,
and the traffic's pulse was no longer beating.
The houses were stiff in the darkness.

A light went on and a window opened,
and suddenly there emerged the lucent warmth
of a trumpet solo.
A song with a strength and joy
that contrasted with the silent streets.
Someone in one of those flats
was lobbing his life towards some place.

Often I think
that only a grief I knew nothing of
could make the melody surge up.
Or that it was my own anguish that made me hear,
in order to survive that night,
something sublime in a few lacklustre notes.

Going back

The moon brings its ancient prestige
to the small, remote rubbish-tip,
now closed-off, that looks down on the valley,
where the lights of a few villages are twinkling.
When we used to come at night
to throw away our rubbish,
we'd stop and gaze at the firmament.
Under the moon, the old rubbish-tip
is today covered in fennel and thyme:
there is the rustle of creatures moving through undergrowth,
owls dazzled by the headlamps of cars.
But it no longer has the power it had
when we'd stand here and gaze,
surrounded by rubbish, at the stars.

The loss of ignorance

Don't write your memoirs.
They'll throw at your feet the person you once were
like an enemy corpse.
When the past begins to be a lie,
it means there's not much left to adopt:
a worthless, futile conviction,
some mistaken cruelty.
Nothing of what must never more be spoken of.
An old man's happiness is silence.

Your street

One shining morning you came here to live.
You are forty-two. The swallows
fly from one end of the street to the other.
There comes a time when structural calculations
reveal the chilly edge of a boundary.
And suddenly you are all alone in the house.
Winter is coming to your street.
Seventy is smiling at you
and you realise it's all very close.
A bus, a metro: you're coming to the sea.

Amarante

It is a village on the Douro, the house is in the square:
one façade looks across at the baroque church
and the other looks right on to the river.
The verandah goes all the way round.
Vende-se, it says on the notice.
I don't write down the telephone number given there.

I have always wanted to go away:
if I travel it is because I am still in pursuit
of some faraway place where I can shelter
and never go back.

The house, the loveliest I have ever seen,
is my last chance.
But I am already far enough away. I don't need to leave.

Vende-se: For sale.

Waking at night

You summon up faces like sheets in the wind
in the lost fields of childhood.
Forget what frightens you, the thing
that made you turn on the light in the early hours.
The fear is not of anyone wanting to leave you
nor of anyone who is no longer here. The fear
is of someone who has never been with you.
Someone who is not ready, yet, to come.

Towards sadness

A wood in the fog
is like sensing memories.
They rise up and fade away
like the path that leads in,
damp with red earth.
I look for the birds
who because of the fog are not singing.
Everything is still: I am already
in the depths of sadness.

There is someone somewhere else
who is reading this poem.
I too am reading you
through these lines of mine,
that your eyes are following.
Among the few places where we can meet
one of them is sadness.

Ocean

We met while walking beside the beach:
I come here to see the sea, I was told.

When I came back
in the gulls' screeching
I hear a woman's voice.

I come here to see the sea:
Facing the waves I say it again.
Inside my head, to nobody.

Bandoneon

We all will be at the port with the Unknown
J.V. FOIX (On the death of Ferrater)

The liturgical harmonium of the street,
Germany's poorest organ,
took ship with those emigrating,
who brought it to the brothels of Buenos Aires.
Like a priest who has apostatised,
it trailed about there among stories
of loneliness and melancholy.
I have always loved tangos. I heard them
when I was a child, on Sunday afternoons,
with my father and mother dancing
up and down the hallway of our house.
They are the voice of an epic that is lost,
with the bandoneon trailing
words that speak of guilty love.
Those who danced them in the hallway
now are only inside a tango.
Strangely happy, an old man sings it
trying out a dance step as he comes closer
with a smile to the Unknown.

Love and survival

Once destroyed, the past is what we always
try to rebuild, like an old country house.
But no one lives there. There is not even the liturgy
that the motorway has, early in the morning.
I understand very little now about those days.
What endures are the consequences. Hard at times.
A dolls' house and the warmth
that hid your loneliness.
Ugly wounds under white bandages.
I walk beneath flawless moons
that shone on your childhood,
I hear a catalogue of stories to send you to sleep.
I think of the dignity of that girl
relinquishing in favour of her sister – so much weaker –
her place as princess. There are no mistakes
that can be made without our realising
as remote as the ones we make over children.
If you don't know which love I am
and if I don't know which love you are
then we must have lost our guiding star.
Although it is many years since I have known anything
of your fears, your hopes
when you find yourself alone in a hotel bedroom,
and I shall never know which of my faces
you will one day choose to remember me by,
I feel, suddenly, that we have survived,
without caresses, an abandonment.

In a small port

The winter sea, when the wind is from the north,
surges in and beats against the jetties with great force.
Abandoned by ships and yachts
the port is surrounded by the breakers' thunder.
Seeing the sea coming in through the harbour mouth,
whipping at the moorings,
I feel the calm that disasters,
once past, leave in their wake.
Happy that today my life
is a little useless winter port,
I turn up the collar of my overcoat, push my fists
into my pockets, weep with joy
and the wind in my face dries my tears for me.

An old man out walking

I wear all the years we have lived together
like a heavy overcoat on a winter's night:
it protects so many hours of grief.
While the darkness freezes waiting for dawn,
there are passing headlights far off. No murderer
can frighten me if I wear the thick coat
beneath which I conceal my love
like a sawn-off shotgun.
I feel the poem in my gut:
a hunger that saves me from death.
There is so much darkness inside each sleeve
that my hands, arthritic and cold,
are now a forgetting or a farewell.

What you take away

I carried my father's ashes around
in the boot of my car
until all of us siblings found a day
to scatter them beneath the fruit trees.
Those trees had awoken in him
a feeling akin to triumph.
Where his people came from the soil was poor.
But there was a kind of poverty
which never abandoned him.
He could not be generous: the fruit
rotted on the trees, he never allowed us
to pick anything but what was on the ground.
When he died, our mother wiped away
the soot of the past, keeping only
the tenderness that some spring or other
managed to bring to those fields.
There we also scattered her ashes.
We siblings quarrelled and sold the field
with the fruit trees, the weeds and the ashes.
There is always something you take away.
You take it with you wherever you go, however bad the place is.

Bat

I don't even believe in music now. I listen to it
bent over, head down in the darkness,
but it is already late, and Mozart is nothing but
this wind from your eyes.
I search in the springtime of dismay
for the woman you once were. I search for her blindly
like the bat which at twilight
imitates the swallow's broken flight.

Restoration

The stone abbey beneath the sun
in summer at midday.
Visitors in respectful groups
explore vast lost spaces,
now rebuilt and well-lit.
But it is a corpse.
There was life here only when the darkness
slid under the arches towards the walls.
Hooded monks, now turned
to red soil beneath some vine,
were building other structures
in their heads. They did it with the sumptuousness
of a now-vanished idea of God.

Restoration means embalming
a stone corpse on August nights,
holiday-makers, concerts, white slacks
and floodlights that illuminate the walls with searing light.
I am an old man and have no wish to be restored.
I know my darkness, the torches and the embers:
there is no brightness other than that of one's own fire.
Under their hoods, the monks knew it.

What are you saying?

Through love and through sex
you have done the only thing that men are capable of doing:
deducing paradise from the fact that the sun rises.
Vaginal dampness: that is all
a man knows of paradise.
Love is also my indifference.
The sun coming up
and the sea being paved with gold and blood
never herald anything.
If something sings within you
cleaving the dark circle of death,
it is childish snatches like: *Oh sun,*
dear little sun, come and see me for I am cold.

Afterwards

Ploughed winter fields: you will gaze at
the tractors which, silently, like insects,
slowly advance towards the horizon.

And my happiness without me.

Mistakes that have saved me from other mistakes:
you will erase the track that brought me
to the common-sense of forgetting.

And my happiness without me.

Woman whom I have desired, smiling:
nights of love without love, the weight of a world
that starts to rub itself out of my eyes.

And my happiness without me.

Light of incompetent loneliness:
you will gaze at an empty stage
illuminating my happy end.

And my happiness without me.

Portrait in blue

Hermitage Museum

His daughter died aged ten,
and now grief does not let his brush
rest while he remembers.
But neither will he paint the future.
What he has painted is helplessness,
the young woman who will never exist.
You have to find words as innocent
and terrible as the blues of Rubens.

Tendencies

We were about twelve, and what I chiefly remember
about that boy is his socks.
White as the moon.
But one day he wore them with a hole,
and under the whiteness his filthy skin could be glimpsed.
Like the worst of the dirt we all carry inside us.
You can't have dealings with anyone
if you don't accept humiliations.

Shelter

The hedge makes the garden.
The rusty vine
and the ivy on the wall.
Clusters of flowers
always waving me goodbye
blown by the breeze.
The hedge makes the garden.
Don't leave it, I implore you:
there are enough who go away
the birds and the moon.
And she who never came back.
The hedge makes the garden.
I understand it is the dead
who give meaning
to this solitude.
And when the sun comes up
each day it fires
a bullet that has been forgotten.
The hedge makes the garden.
Not any old hedge: the hedge
which, protecting the roses,
protects me also.

The final meaning

It is misty and night-time. Unable to sleep I see
all the darkness that is waiting for me
perched like a bird on top of what I have lost.
I have opened the window. The mist is thinning.
I could never forget all that I owe you:
the final meaning of the word love.
Brutal in its precision, the night sky.

The collapsed roof

The tiles jumbled
with cement and plaster,
the joists like bones
on the plate after a meal.
The collapsed roof
now speaks the same
language as the rain.
A background of darkness underfoot,
where everything is underground.

Journey

I am thinking of you from a train
that has stopped in a station
of a town where I have never been.
It is a station with weary platforms.
Difficult at dusk.
When time is draining away,
it is as desolate as one may dare to dream.

The train pulls out and passes in front of some houses.
They are right beside the tracks. A window is lit
revealing the room within: it is one instant
with the blurred suspicion of lives.
And it is barely more than this, what I know
of what we have always called our love.

A window in Marià Cubí Street

I met him around the time of *The steps of the hunter.*
I don't know whether we were friends. He could just as well
       have been
the tenderness that comes from helplessness
as the conceitedness that comes with fear.
Generous but at the same time irascible and untruthful.
A certain desperation united us:
him for his grandson, me for my daughter.
He constantly denied reality,
the more so the more the battle was lost.
I came to love him. I like his poetry
very much when it evokes
through the eyes of a man or a woman
the silence of fields where there is no one.
He fell scything the air, with a dull blow.
A parody of the bird
brought down by the hunter's shot.

In memoriam José Agustín Goytisolo, Spanish poet and author
of books like *The steps of the hunter.*

New day

Dawn burns the leaves
with its actress eyes.
My dead, my exile:
tell me something,
tell me the whole of this
marvellous story.
I have to set light to the firewood:
dry wood of disgust,
fear, loneliness,
and even oblivion,
in order to burn all the wrong
years of the abyss.
The lonely house
that I have become
now has no other door
but that of happiness.

The last unknown place

At seventy he still remembers
his childish dream,
the hot water in a metal bowl
and that red-haired girl bathing him.
The eyes, the skin, the lips, the smell girls have.
Later, his youth, with the depth
of touch and a story that was lost
before it began. Always her body,
silent and mythical, a half-open door
he never stepped through.
He did not know where it led until very late,
in the gaze of an older woman.
With that he has enough. He enters shocked
by happiness, and senses how her eyes
behind the wall of desire are gazing at him
in this last unknown place.

Tenerife

I was sixteen: in the early morning
I would open my bedroom window
on to that calm, colonial city.
I gazed at the modest lights beside such a dark sea.

Life has already gone by.
Other lights have come on in another city.
I look into your eyes and I begin again.
In the background, darkness, as if it were the sea.

Distant memory

Bent over the plough,
he pressed down hard to push
the ploughshare deep into the ground.
When the mule stopped
to piss, instead of hitting it
to make it go on, he said to me:
you have to let the mule piss
because when it pisses, it has a rest.
Life meant setting
the blade and opening the furrows.
Setting his compassionate
gaze on a mule
at the end of the war.
May someone remember in this way –
profound and compassionate –
one of my poems.

Café interior

In a mirror on the opposite wall
there is my face, that stares back at me, on my own
as though watching the trains of childhood pass.
We used to live in a small dark flat
near the station. I lived on my own
with my mother and father's hot fear
and a dead sister.

But in the background,
in the mirror's winter, through the window,
I see the tracks covered in snow.
I know what is happening to me. I am beginning to be happy.

Talking of architecture

There were few people still living in the village,
and the house had been used as a barn
since the end of the war.
We began setting it to rights,
and now we have given it a new roof
built on top of the old one, with a good gable-end.
What have we destroyed, what house am I talking about,
and what detestable architecture
has life irremediably ended up being?
You can no longer see the past through the windows.

Textual criticism

There were not two lovers in Valencia like us
VICENT A. ESTELLÉS, 'The lovers'

Well of course there were other lovers like them in Valencia.
And throughout the world. I can even remember some.
It is hard to say whether it is so wonderful
when you are young to roll about all day on the ground
and afterwards spend years pining for the battle.
Life is neither a comfortable nor a kindly matter.
Rather it is dry and completely impersonal:
a fire that may be confused with light.
There is nothing else. If there is,
it runs through Bécquer, Larkin, Petrarch, people like that.
And – in this we agree – neither is it any great matter.
How I remember you, Vicent, selfish, a prey
to sickness, ailments, mingling pieces of impudence
with quotations from Ausiàs March.
In fact it was a mental effort to turn yourself over.
Just as Bécquer, Petrarch and Larkin do.
And you in your poem, good, if I remove the final line.
We live always through sex. We are lucky
to want it, have it, and also to remember it,
regret having had it, and regret losing it.
Sex and words. The loneliness of the world.

This is a commentary on a classic Catalan poem which
ends with the line: *because very few lovers like us were born.*

112

Room in the Students' Residence

There is a chestnut tree filling the windows' space.
It caresses the glass with leaves
that curl as they dry.
While I am looking at this golden morning,
I think of someone who, one distant autumn,
came to live here, maybe in this very room.
Now he is dust glowing in the rays of the sun.
Life has left me free
to fall like the leaves.
November brings happiness close
to this old maker of structural calculations.
If death has not come,
the first frosts will find him more solitary.
It is too late now to try to understand.

Landscape

We have reached this final refuge.
Here begins
what you might perhaps call loneliness.
The first step in forgetting who we are
and keeping each other company at the very foot
of the icy rock that keeps watch over us.
Everything is there in our eyes.
And the thaw, a river as far as death.
There was little, very little needed, in order to be happy.

Raquel

A name for you alone:
a name that caresses
a woman's naked body
and brings it close to my lips.
A name for you alone,
to see in your eyes
the terrace being watered
and the ivy poisoned
by moonlight.
A name for you alone
who, harsh as ivy,
accused the poem
of being cruel, and only
wanted kindness.
A name for you alone.
A word made of air
above a field of flowers.

Victory

While listening to the wind I turn on the radio.
I listen to a young woman complaining
about a power cut: she says it left her
without domestic appliances, *like centuries ago.*
Like centuries ago.
It's little enough I know of the place I come from,
it's very little I know about the sea's brutality
where fishermen in their hunger hoisted the tuna
with hooks out of a sea splashed with blood
so that a tiny, tough young girl
could study to be a teacher and be my mother.

I listen to the wind against the dry earth.
What awaits us. Flies. Like centuries ago.

After rain

There is a sad, weary time
that buries itself in my memory
while I look out nostalgically
at the happiness of the fields.
I breathe in the green smell
that comes up from the earth.
Pain weighs me down just like
mud on my shoes.

Warmth

Death has cut across my life.
Just as when I was a child, when, slowly
the furrier's cart would cross the village.
I saw death as she passed
with the rabbit skins, grey and soft.
I am an ill-starred wall
in which only one window opens.
The last spot from which the sun retreats.

Cold on the beach

Gulls soar
slow and grey
gulls of evening.
But it is midday.
I look at the girls
on the sand,
old flags
with which life
still persists
in sending me signals.
Illusions:
how you have wearied me.

Well-being

Rain falls on the sunflowers
that bend their dark heads towards the earth.
They are like fields of words, drenched
with rain, that protect the fallen birds of the future.
On time's face, a smile of thanks
lingers. Gazing out of the window,
an old man stands, feeling the chill of the glass
against which, with the murmur of drums,
the rain has beaten all night.
He desires nothing now, he smiles
because, when the future dies, the past dies also.
He is like another among all these sunflowers
who bend their dark heads towards the earth.

Another oracle

Facing the white wind-turbines with their metallic sheen,
the sun is setting in the clear winter air.
I think of the time when there were none.
Slowly I come to understand that those were the days
of broader horizons. Now they rise up
from their site, brutal things, these "windmills"
orientated towards a difficult time.
I get close to one of them and feel its indifference.
I stroke its huge icy foot,
I hear the future in the powerful language
of a scythe slicing the air with its great blades.
They whirl furiously, face to the setting sun,
like someone who might tell the truth.

Calm

It is not hard to imagine she has returned
like the moon in the night.
It is a children's story. The yellow leaves
are the words that November speaks
until it shapes a lime tree that shines
among the dark green of the other trees.
It is our clear autumn night
with the moon in the story about this tree.
I sing the burning leaf of night's gold.
The last leaf, her testimony
on the lime tree's highest branch.

Night at the year's end

The dark chill of the windows
looks down on a dirty
narrow street in Rome.
It is an unpretentious hotel
with red moquette carpets
which almost stifle
the noise of celebration.
Each of us two is reading
under his or her lamp.
In a gilded mirror
the room is forgetting us.

Arrivederci, Roma.
We old ones are saying goodbye
to cities for ever.

Sonata

While I listen, the rain is falling.
I think of the solitary dog, trotting
behind Mozart's hearse: I can follow it
in the piano's tempo and, at the same time,
in the paths the water makes on the glass.
Strangely happy, I follow a dog
made of rain and of music.

A corner of the mind

They are images of frightened children.
The sad little face in the steamed-up glass of a bus,
the face grimy with tears whom you find
wandering along a street, the eyes
already hardened by morphine
that gaze up at you from a bed.

They emerge from the half-shadows of a corner
that is the warmest shelter of the mind.
All the lost children are coming home.

Youth

Love takes on the shape of vermin
when it runs from our bed.
I cherish the memory of a pair of soft, warm feet.
I will describe them on the blank pages
of your future diaries.
I have not forgotten those years: they are the heat
that the sun will no longer have.
Dangerous memories,
and I must write a poem about a wolf
caught in a trap in the snow.

Early morning story

It is raining on the empty square.
There is a single taxi at the taxi-rank.
The driver's wait is a long one.
He has turned off the engine and it is very cold.
A door opens, a rain-soaked passenger,
tired, bad-tempered: he gives an address.
When they go through a red light, he shouts at him.
Turning round, the driver murmurs:
It is a week since my son died.
Silenced, the passenger sinks back in his seat.
Later on that night, when a group of passengers
board, making a racket, he tells them:
It is a week since my son died.
We've all got to die, they reply,
amid clumsy jokes and guffaws.
Comes the time to sign off, back at the garage,
he goes across to the radio-hut:
It is a week since my son died.
Her eyes red with fatigue, *Yes,*
the woman replies, while she attends to the voices
emanating with other sounds from the transmitter.

This is, in fact, one of Chekhov's stories.
There it is a coach with a horse, and it is snowing.
I know the taxi-driver will not be able to sleep.
Is death inside the fist raised by life?
Or else, is death the fist in which we are grasped?
In Chekhov's story, the coachman
will still have the horse in whom he'll confide
that his son has died. All at once I feel it

inside me, and that fear is turning to ice,
and I light a fire to warm us all,
the taxi-driver, the coachman, me and my dead,
you who are reading me
and Chekhov, and all together we see how life
falls, like snow, in solitude.
A night train, washed with pink,
at dawn crosses the olive groves.
Here – weary, full of sleep and, at the same time,
strangely happy – I end this poem.

The last evening

I have never seen another like it,
with the end-of-spring light
coming into the house, among the people.
So still, you seemed pensive.
The time yet to come
did not dare to enter an air
that would not resign itself to being sad.
We were still upheld
by the faint smile on your cold lips.
It was the last evening that love
was able to hold the high ground.
Unstoppable, later,
grief and death overtook it.

Avec le temps

There were these rocks beside the sea
and a twisting pine tree
firmly rooted in a crack.
While I walk in the winter sun
along the stony beach, I see the rocks,
but, now, with no trace of any pine.
I have picked up a pebble.
There is no surer warmth
than the mineral heat of stone in the sun.
I'm coming, I murmured as I threw it
into a sea as blue as that summer's.

The dark beneath the white

Snow was covering the city. Today
I wonder whether we were wrong
or if lives are always like that.
The dark beneath the white.
Snow was covering the city.
So cold and always a part of our love.
The white calm will never return
again with the print of our feet.
The future already lay beneath the snow.

Summer evening

I watch the eagle flying.
Taking its time
it goes skating
over the lake of the sky.
What hunter
would want to shoot it down
from high above the fields?
I am the quarry
and the hunter.

The eagle flies
over my past.
It hovers without moving
and in an instant,
like a stone
it plummets downwards
smashing the sky's
pinks and purples,
shattering it
like a stained-glass window.

I want to keep you
alive and near me,
but jealous
death lets itself
plummet in silence
steeply down.
It goes back to searching for you
in my memory.

The prodigal son begins his return

I gaze through the window in the darkness
at the smaller house in the road.
A street-lamp that shines all night
throws a patch of yellow light
on the hostile silence of the pavement.
Coming back is love if someone is waiting for you.
Going away when no one comes to welcome you is death.
It is not long now till dawn.
Feelings take root in a place
where there is nothing left.
The light thrown by the street-lamp pales
as day begins to break.
In the half-light a dog crosses
the last street in the village. It goes off towards the outskirts.
As I go off to where the houses peter out.

Childhood park

The moonlight glides
over the well-mown grass.
There is a child playing at hiding
in the darkness of childhood.
And a barefoot old man who searches for him
feeling the chill of the lawn
that is wet with dew.

Sunset

Like stars above you and soon above me
R.M. RILKE

Every day you are further off.
This is what the red gleamings.
that varnish the sea tell me.
Later on, when they darken,
the gaze lifts
towards the blue of twilight.
I have grown used to living
with you who are no longer here.
Above you, the stars.
Soon above me.

Forès, 2008

I spent a lot of time on my own as a child,
and now life returns me to that place
where without haste I am able, like the birds,
to feel that distance is in my eyes.
Solitude at last, which I share
with an old woman who is in love
inside her own night, likewise with no one.
The newspapers on an armchair
are like a companionable pet
that is indifferent and asleep. Solitude
commemorates nothing. It is a geography.

Hokusai

It was my father who introduced me
to painting. He did it through magazines,
well-printed ones, from that lost place
we called – and still call – the Republic.
I drew and painted for some years
with the futile rage of the convert.
It was as though I lived inside the paintings
of the lonely Museum of Modern Art
where there was never anyone. It resembled
a French provincial city.
And suddenly, there was the first Hokusai.
Slanting lines completely erasing a bridge
and men and women with umbrellas.
Now that I am old I would like to live
inside one of these Hokusai landscapes.
May they protect me as I cross my bridge,
those swift, tense, slanting lines.
The delicate grilles of the rain.

Line 4: The Spanish Republic destroyed by Franco.

137

Ballad of the sorrows

Seeing you are here no longer,
I, with all my sorrows joined,
made myself a grief of iron.

So there should not also be lost
the part of you that may endure,
night is soldering with darkness
the entire circle of the moon.

Slowly then this life of ours
is entering the poems I write.
Within them it will wait for you.

Reading poetry

Finishing this book of poems by Paul Celan,
I don't know what he has told me
nor what he wanted to tell me. I don't even know
if he was claiming to tell me anything.
The hermetic poets are afraid.
I place my hand on the cover of the book
and I swear to abjure that fear for ever.
For poetry, which sometimes begins
by being a landscape where we arrive at night,
ends up always being a mirror
in which we read our own lips.
What meaning does the skip have if it is empty?
Silence and emptiness are for the angels.
For the fear of filth and rubbish
or for the filth and rubbish of fear.

Muntaner Street

Clifford Brown, 'Summertime'

The blood-curdling noise
of those iron trams
that hurled themselves down the hill
was already music to me.

That was many years ago. Life
has been this long concert.
It has left the scores
on music-stands that are wire
fences left behind
on an old battle field.

But sometimes I am still
rescued by the dissonance
of a jazz trumpet.
It hits the top notes,
almost losing pitch,
like the trams' solo
while, at top speed,
they went down Muntaner
careering towards a dangerous
iron sea of happiness.

Last books

The garden was just a field of weeds
and she a child: she wasn't yet walking.
I planted the poplar:
it was just a bare branch, straight and slender.
Now it is like a five-storey house,
with dense, dark-green, shining foliage.
It rises up from the lawn, and I can no longer
wrap my arms around its trunk.
Nor shall I ever embrace her again.
Keeping pace with life, death also grows.
There remains just one possibility:
to understand the word *last*,
an open place with no possibility of plunder.
The happiness of never going back.

The Navy (1950)

When the vessels of the Sixth Fleet
began to make Barcelona a stop over,
the Rambla's colour of defeat
began to shine a little. The sailors
in their white uniforms brought jazz
to the gloomy streets of the *Barri Xino*.
I remember how at night in the *Cafè de l'Òpera*
a venerable-looking elderly man
would give English lessons to a few whores.
There were long queues on the jetty
where the launches left to go out to the aircraft-carrier,
the huge, grey, iron Iliad
anchored in the offing facing the port.
It was a good fleet. It had destroyed
Japan's armada and Germany's too.
I can still feel it inside me.
I didn't realise then that each one of us
spends our life fabricating the myths
that are to defend us from our terrors.
After sixty years,
on this peaceful evening in New York,
I have been remembering that aircraft-carrier
that still for me has all its lights lit
though facing a darker port.
And I go back to being that child
who read those children's comics about the Second World War,
where the Americans were the good guys,
and I stared at the girls in their thin dresses
who went laughing, arm-in-arm with the sailors in white.
The myth carries on to reach *The Village Vanguard*,

where a black sax is playing. Black and old,
as old as the one in the *Cafè de l'Òpera*.
As old as the sailors are now
and the girls, if they aren't already dead.
The myth carries on into the hotel room,
where I am doing accounts with my epoch
which is over, leaving me on my own.

Barri Xino: Chinese quarter. But not because there were Chinese
residents. It was a poor, densely populated quarter in Barcelona,
famous for prostitution, night life, etc.

Lunch at *Los Pinos*

What happiness to wake up on Sundays
with the light like an older sister
and your arms, the cross of my desire.
They were mornings that have never ceased
to stream through the window. Barcelona,
when it was poor, humble, welcoming
as cities are when they have been lonely,
smiled beyond the window panes.
We stayed in bed until midday
and went to have lunch at that restaurant
in the pinewood, at the foot of Tibidabo.
Back then, there was no need
to put a name to what we did.
Sleeping together, love, sex and pain
were all one and the same: what we were.

Time howls but does so in silence
like a wolf with cancer of the throat.
Nothing belongs to me. All at once,
in this unknown city
I can defend nothing but the room where now,
strangely happy, I listen to the sound
of Ben Webster's unhurried sax.
Wrapped in an old newspaper
I still keep the rose of many years ago:
that more complicated Barcelona
where my life was searching for its place.

Fragility

Out of the tear that is home to your absence
the intimate north wind carries a memory
far out to sea, and in its violence
overturns tables at the bar, now empty.

Anguish remains like a presence:
seven years of the usual places, without you,
have turned themselves into an epic
about a single character, a pure sorrow.

A pure sorrow with that which, smiling,
I'll put an end to, dying of grief.
Many times have I tried to imagine

that you are simply far away. I try again.
While I drink my coffee, I burnish the dream
as the wind does the enormous blue of the sea.

Bed scene for Eugene O'Neill

They have uttered some phrases that may,
or may not, be true. They don't care.
They have turned off the light. There is nothing they want.
In their expression, a dry sadness,
devoid of melancholy or nostalgia,
like the look in the eyes of the fox when it stares,
hungrily, at the empty ploughland.

Order

In memoriam Ángel González, Spanish poet

They are scarcely the faces of love.
I see them as they emerge
from the half-light of a very old fear.
I mix up the living and the dead, because losses –
like lamps in a bedroom –
give life to my privacy.
I need this order. It is like living
inside Hemingway's shortest short story:
A Clean, Well-Lighted Place.
That is what your poetry has been for me:
a clean, well-lighted place.

Sant Francesc de Borja

Alonso Cano, Museo de Bellas Artes, Seville

The dark habit takes up the entire picture,
and at the top the lit half-face
of the man who said:
I will serve no master who must die.
The eye that the shadow does not cover, hard and black,
is that of a bird of prey: it is looking at
the iron crown of his prince,
which a hand amid his robe is gripping
as though he had picked it up off the ground. The eye
violently scorns the iron.
It is an obsession with eternity
which hates what is ephemeral and will not admit
that love exists because footprints
left in the snow disappear.

Hotel

In the empty lobby, the big window
has the sadness of trees at nightfall
and a weariness of cars and of people.
I think how you are not with me and how this is Lisbon:
when I was young, with little more than this
I would have written a love poem.
But the lights coming on, the gale,
the traffic and the people rushing blindly
as though with some idea where they are going, evoke for me
how difficult it has been, our life together.
Each of us carries this sadness
that comes from the other, and doesn't know what to do with it.
Maybe love is just that. And missing you
in the window – darker every moment –
of a hotel where I don't know why I have come.
Maybe just to be far away from you.

Experience of a fatherland

Beneath the radiant summer afternoon
we were scrambling up some rocks beside the sea,
me, hiding my fear of heights, proud
of this complicity with my father.
But then he trod on that nest.
The wasps in their rage poured out
in my direction, where I was climbing behind him.
Pell-mell down the rocks to throw myself into the sea,
covered in stings to the face and arms,
a child confronted by horror.
He stood without moving, gripping
the rock where the nest was, on top of the crag.

How lonely the afternoon was,
the blue and pink afternoon that comes back to me
from Port de la Selva, nineteen-fifty.
We have inherited a furious environment,
classical, brutish, sad, with nests of wasps
that have always flown out against poets.

The old man and Death

The December rains cause faces
to share winter's physiognomy.
I come out to greet you on the wet pavement.
You didn't need to say anything because I knew who you were.
Once inside the house you take off your overcoat:
you're wearing trainers and jeans, with a blouse.
No ring.
A preliminary visit, you murmur.
On the final visit we shall not speak.
You look around you and see the book
still open on the table: *Rilke?*
Do you like the poem about Leda?
Today I am her and you are the swan.
I don't see it like that, I reply. You are who you are
and I, more like 'The leper king',
because now that I'm old I put my trust in you:
I may attain a fresh dignity.
Now you no longer do me harm. You arrive,
with no fuss, and you shatter words
like fine but useless china.

You know I have lived but you don't know why
and you don't understand that I may be speaking of motives.
You'll soon find out how little they matter,
you say impatiently without looking at me.
You look like my mother, I'm thinking. Cold,
worried about me, too strict:
I seem to recognise in you the bitterness
she felt at not knowing how to love me.

As though I were here talking to you
in one of those moments from childhood,
both of us playing at being in nineteen-thirty-eight.
Wrapped in grey smoke, trains are pulling
their iron wagons that crash into each other.
There are still a lot of carts, fires in the hearth,
shadows concealing every corner.
Machado was here, here they locked
my grandfather up in prison, here he saw me
for the first and last time.
You are far away in spite of the bombings and the influenza.
I have always been right beside you. You don't realise
how ordinary dying is, you say seriously.
To be more precise, ordinary and lonely.

You wander through the house, looking
at rooms, at the furniture, the windows.
You keep stopping in front of photographs.
No greater complicity than that of sex
for this poor domestic cruelty,
you say slyly as I realise that your shadow
pours from your décolletage. To be old
is to understand the sex of death.
I know that story, you reply:
that talk of death and sex. You have been
struggling desperately all your life
against being one, but you are a melancholic.
It's no good: you're just a prisoner,
and, squalidly, all the furniture around you
has kept its eye on you, ever since you were a child,
and I myself inside the chest-of-drawers,
throughout your life among the underwear.

My iron mind has turned to rust
within the Jewish and Christian crater
where the executed Christ grows dark,
he whom with the sponge soaked in vinegar
we try to sustain with a thread of life
while we wait for signs from the darkness
that will never come. *It is a story
without meaning, that attempts to deny me*, you say.
And suddenly you become hospitable.
Why is it so hard that nothing should be waiting for us?
And now I do see quenched in your eyes
the slow depth of a smile.
I know what you're laughing at, I tell you. *You don't know*, you reply.
You cannot know what it is death laughs at.
All that a woman ever found in me
comes back into my eyes as though to an animal's,
but threatening, and huge, and apart.
And the animal comes to you to be stroked
and to lick your soft, cold hands.
*You are mistaken if you are searching
for an epic that may give some meaning
to my ordinary and impersonal actions.
Remember those busts of heroes fallen
in the Great War*, you say sharply,
*with their cloaks and tired eyes made of bronze
gazing at the horizon of their failure.
You transform, as they transformed, reverence into the loathsome.*
And you fall silent, and I am inside the silence
gazing through you at the future
which, sightless and with no lips, smiles at me.

We have been silent for a while. In 'The prodigal son'
Rilke pours out his reluctance over leaving.

153

Going away, I think. And you look at me. You guess
what I do not utter only through self-respect.
And very slowly you recite the final line:
Is this the gateway to a new life?
Already I begin to feel you within me
like the lights of a shack in the forest.
My voice, when by then I shall no longer hear it,
will fade like the echo of the shot
from a hunter across the fields. I can see there
in your eyes the silence that will remain afterwards.
And suddenly the desperate barking,
already pointless, of the dogs.
To understand is to trust in the one who is near
appealing to the past as a refuge.
And everything – including myself – is part of a long
and precise formula which ends 'equal to zero'.
You say it in a tired voice, adding:
I am the final gift. You will honour me by your silence.
What tenderness hidden there, I think.
And I question you: God? *Yes*, you reply:
A shape time takes. And Orpheus? I ask,
leaving Hades in front of his Eurydice,
what did he see when he looked back?
Nothing, Eurydice was nothing
but the void at the centre of his life,
very carefully wrapped in that name.

The child of waste ground, I have fathered
more waste ground. Now, lucidity
is the throbbing of grief in the darkness.
I say this, but am quickly halted
by the mockery in your eyes: I think I have spoken
the word grief too many times,
and now it means only the stones

which someone, down the years, has thrown into the sea.
A reading-lamp sheds its light
on the open book upon the table.
Nothing will shatter my consciousness
as when I go off with you in the black car.
The one in the poem 'The abduction',
clothed in the cold and the night when, as I get in,
I shall hear you in the darkness: I am with you.

Soon, all that will be left is a word –
silence – with which to write this poem.
And to forget you. And myself.

And through my veins oblivion will run.
I am boring you, telling you what you already know,
but you are the remedy for something,
I tell you, and you make a gesture of indifference,
while, like a storm, the weariness
fades from my words and disappears.
I don't know where you are taking me. *Why do you care?* you say.
Because, wherever it is you're taking me, there is someone I love.
Oh, it's not a place, you reply,
and in your dead eyes there appears suddenly
the look I loved so much.
Your past is leaving with me, you explain,
and life begins to feel uncomfortable,
as when the wind gets up in a garden.
You have been destroyed in me, but you have been wandering
lost for a long time. How late it always is.
And, getting up, you say: *life has meaning*
because it comes to an end and, as in a poem,
the most difficult part is always the ending.
You should know that. Then:
No need to come with me, I know the way. You too.

155

Love that does not frighten me

Far from the fierce love of the source,
far from the love the mind invents as a refuge,
the love that consoles me now has no urgency.
Warm, respectful: the love of the winter sun.
To love is to discover some promise
of rehearsal that is calming.

These poems speak of writing.
Because love is always an affair
of the final pages.
There is no ending that can attain
the height of such loneliness.